USSY UMAR

Hands-On Lab Exercises for Cisco Networking Beginners

Building A Practical Networking Skills from the Ground Up

Copyright © 2024 by Ussy Umar

All rights reserved. No part of this publication may be reproduced, stored or transmitted in any form or by any means, electronic, mechanical, photocopying, recording, scanning, or otherwise without written permission from the publisher. It is illegal to copy this book, post it to a website, or distribute it by any other means without permission.

First edition

Contents

1	Introduction	1
2	LAB 1: EIGRP Configuration	2
3	LAB 2: EIGRP Authentication	3
4	LAB 3: Static Neighborship in Eigrp	4
5	LAB 4: EIGRP Metric Tuning	5
6	LAB 5: Route-filtering using distribute-list with a standard...	7
7	LAB 6: Route-filtering using distribute-list with an...	9
8	LAB 7 :Route-filtering using distribute-list with a...	11
9	LAB 8: Route-filtering using distribute-list with an IP...	13
10	LAB 9: Route Summarization	15
11	LAB 10: EIGRP Default Routing	16
12	LAB 11: Unequal Cost Load Balancing	17
13	LAB 12: OSPF Authentication	19
14	LAB 13: MD5 Authentication	20
15	LAB 14: OSPF Point-to-Point Network	21
16	LAB 15: OSPF Broadcast Network	22
17	LAB 16: OSPF Non-Broadcast Multi Access (NBMA) network	24
18	LAB 17: OSPF point to Multipoint network	26
19	LAB 18: Configure OSPF Point-to-Multipoint Non-Broadcast...	28
20	LAB 19: OSPF metric tuning	30
21	LAB 20: OSPF Stub and totally stub area	32
22	LAB 21: NSSA and Total NSSA	34
23	LAB 22: Summarization at ABR	36
24	LAB 23: Summarization at ASBR	37
25	LAB 24: Default Routing in OSPF	39
26	LAB 25: OSPF Virtual link with no authentication.	40

27	LAB 26: OSPF Virtual link with authentication.	42
28	LAB 27: OSPF (NNSA)	44
29	LAB 28: OSPF Manual Configuration	46
30	LAB 29: Redistribution of EIGRP into OSPF	48
31	LAB 30: EIGRP over Frame-Relay	50
32	LAB 31: EIGRP and OSPF	52
33	LAB 32: OSPF over Frame Relay	54
34	LAB 33: OSPF Type	56
35	LAB 34: Source Based Routing	58
36	LAB 35: EIGRP over Frame-Relay using point-to-multipoint	60
37	LAB 36: BGP	61
38	LAB 37: Redistribution to OSPF	63
39	LAB 38: RIP over FRAME RELAY	65
40	LAB 39: EIGRP SUCCESSOR AND FEASIBLE	67
41	LAB 40: OSPF NSSA And Redistribution	69
42	LAB 41: RIPv2	71
43	LAB 42: RIP, EIGRP Redistribution	73
44	LAB 43: OSPF ROUTE	75
45	LAB44: VLAN (VIRTUAL LAN)	77
46	LAB 45: Trunking with ISL encapsulation	79
47	LAB46: Trunking with ISL encapsulation using Dynamic...	81

1

Introduction

Starting on the journey to master networking requires hands-on practice to grasp core concepts and develop essential skills. A practice lab for Cisco networking beginners is a crucial resource designed to provide immersive, real-world experiences. Exercises covering basic topics like IP addressing, subnetting, VLANs, and basic router and switch configuration are usually included in these labs. These exercises provide novices with the opportunity to apply theoretical knowledge, troubleshoot common issues, and develop self-confidence by simulating real network environments. Learners can build a strong foundation in networking through organized, step-by-step tasks, which will prepare them for advanced certifications and challenges in the workplace.

2

LAB 1: EIGRP Configuration

TASK: Build a neighborship relationship between R1 and R2 in order to form a relationship between them, Configure the loopbacks as their router id.

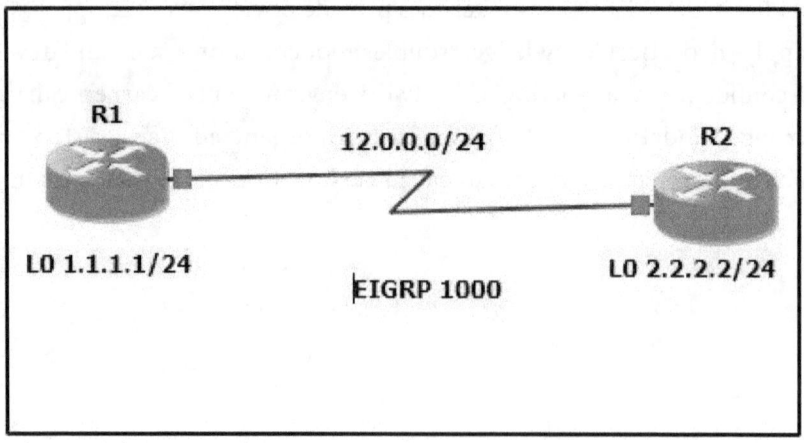

3

LAB 2: EIGRP Authentication

Tasks: Configuring authentication between R1 and R2 to authenticate Eigrp messages.

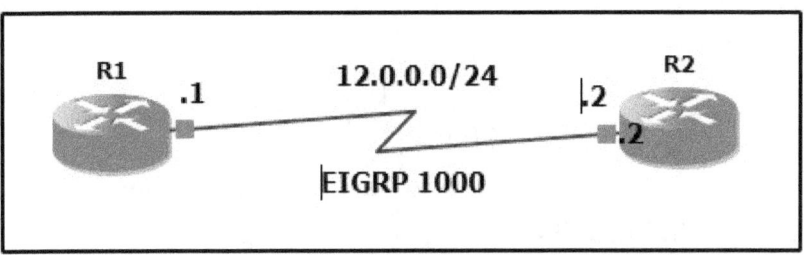

4

LAB 3: Static Neighborship in Eigrp

TASK: Static Neighborship: Defining static neighborship between R1-R2 and R1-R3 using frame-relay over EIGRP without the broadcast keyword.

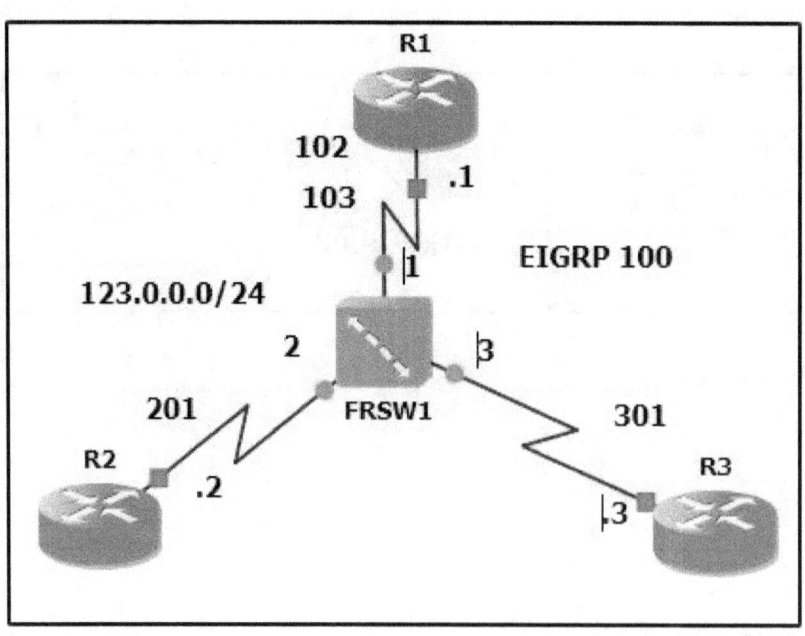

5

LAB 4: EIGRP Metric Tuning

The best route for the network 172.168.30.0/24 of R3 from R1 is via R2. The task is to make the route via R4 and R5 best for the network 172.168.30.0/24 of R3 from R1.

Task:

1. Configure metric values and to make the path via R4 and R5 as the best path for the network of R3 from R1.
2. Use an offset list and to make the path via R4 and R5 as the best path for the network of R3 from R1.

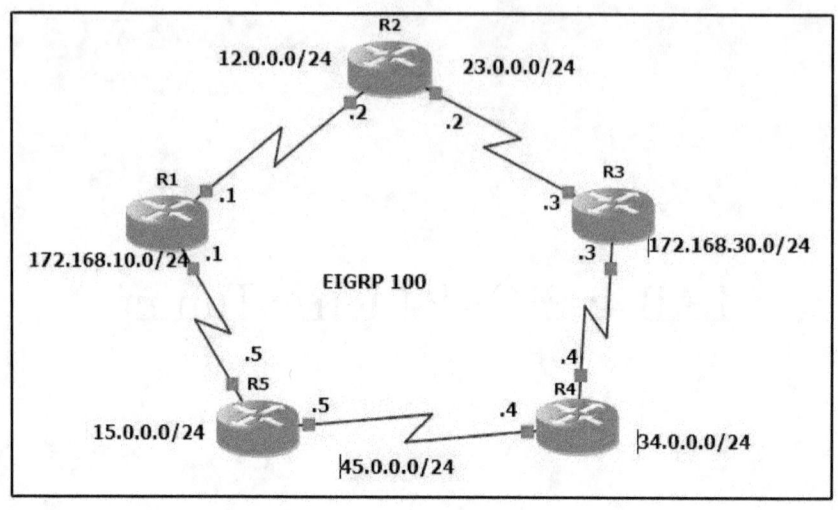

6

LAB 5: Route-filtering using distribute-list with a standard ACL

Task: The task specifies using distribute-lists and standard access control lists (ACLs) to filter loopback networks of Router 4 (R4) from the routing table of Router 2 (R2) and Router 3 (R3).

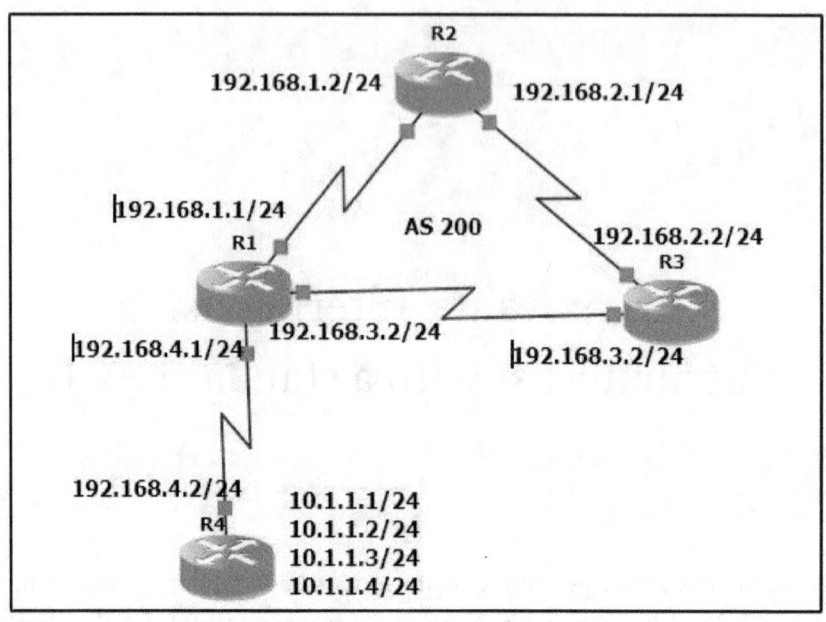

7

LAB 6: Route-filtering using distribute-list with an extended ACL

Task: The task involves filtering loopback networks of Router 2 (R2) from the routing table of Router 3 (R3) using distributed lists and extended ACLs.

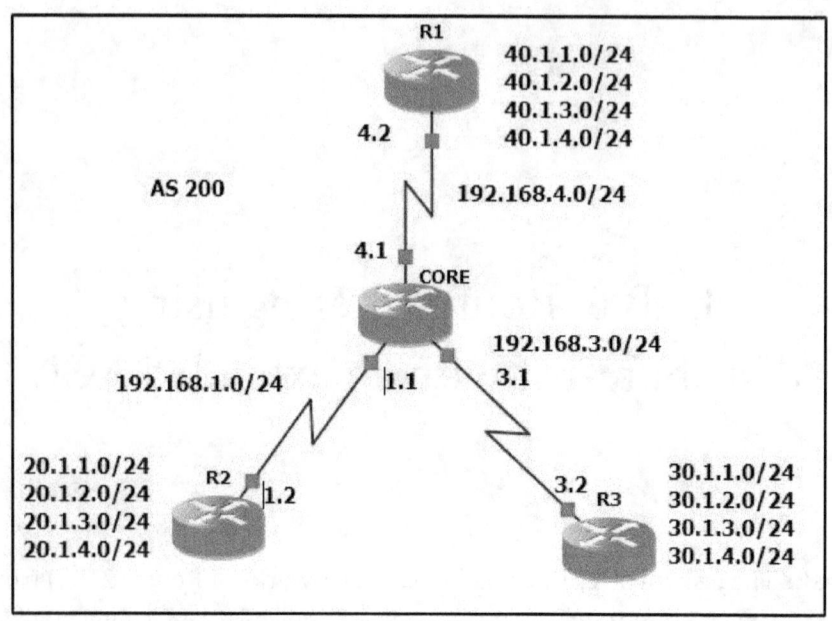

8

LAB 7 : Route-filtering using distribute-list with a Route-map

Task: To filter the loopback networks of R2 from the routing table of R3 using distribute-list with a route-map.

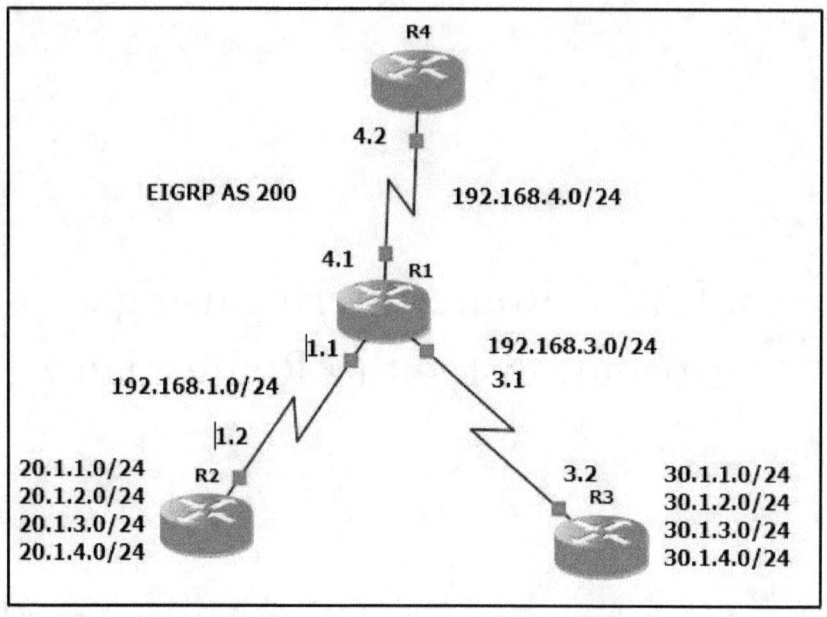

9

LAB 8: Route-filtering using distribute-list with an IP prefix-list

Task: Filter routes from R3 in R2's routing table using an IP prefix-list.

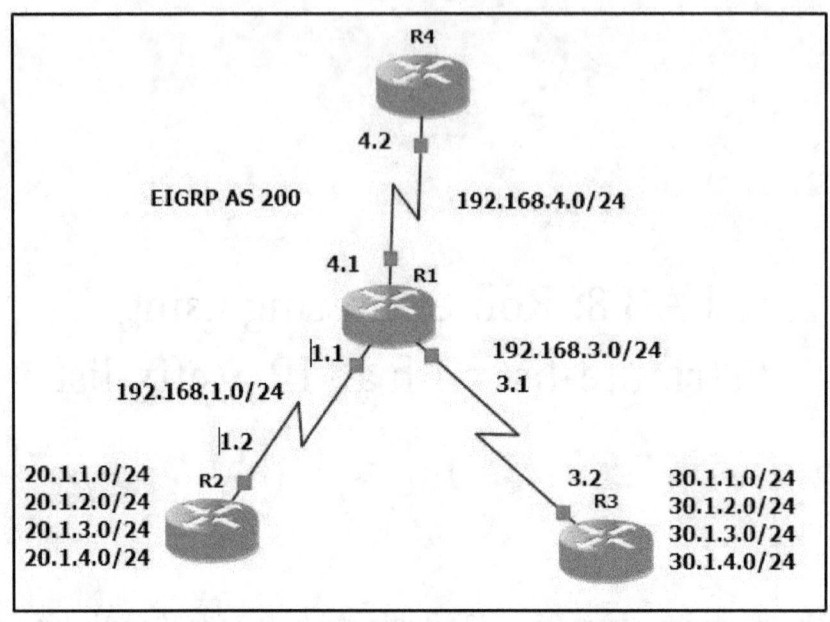

10

LAB 9: Route Summarization

Task: To summarize routes of all the branches so that the core will get only summary routes of all the branches instead of individual routes.

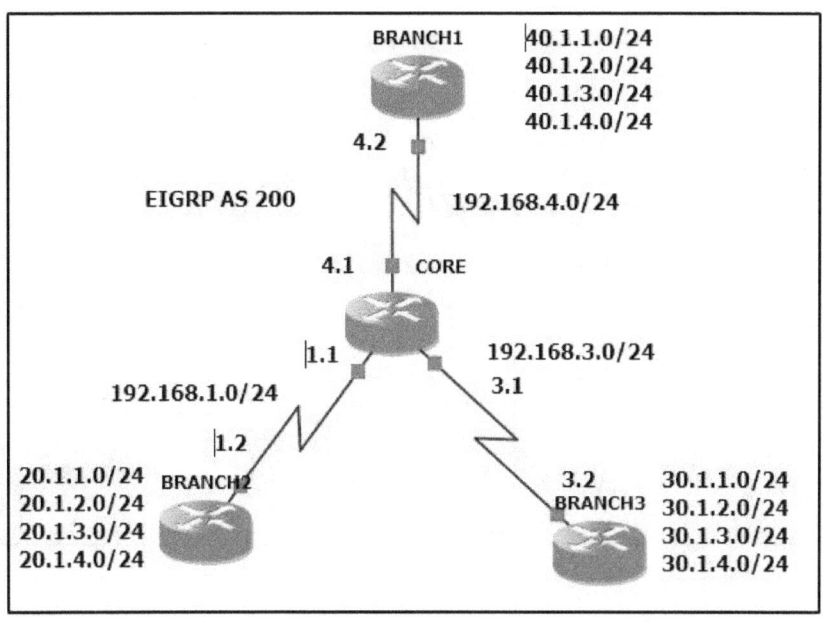

11

LAB 10: EIGRP Default Routing

Task Configure default routing on R1 to perform routing between two different AS (AS 100 and AS 200) of the EIGRP.

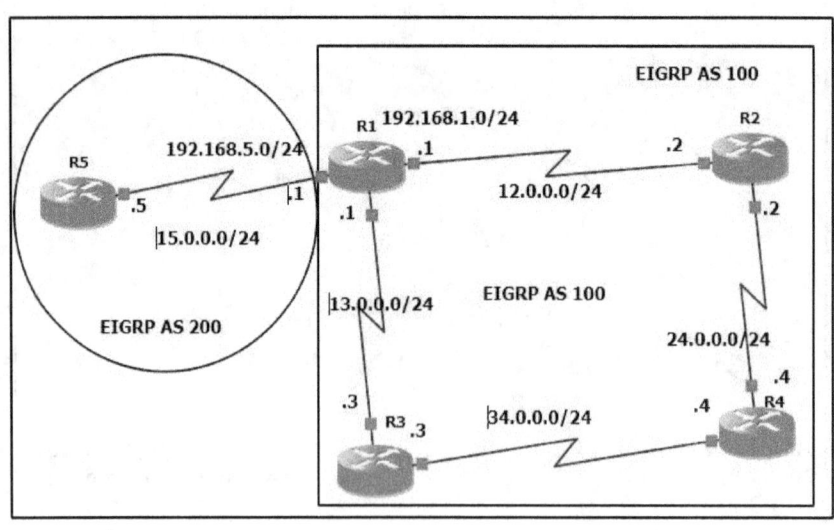

12

LAB 11: Unequal Cost Load Balancing

Task: By default R1 is receiving all loopback networks of R3 from its neighbor R2. So whenever R1 will send any traffic towards loopback interfaces of R3 it will follow the path via R2. However, R1 has two links towards the R3 network. Now the user wants to perform load balancing on both of the existing links for the network of R3.

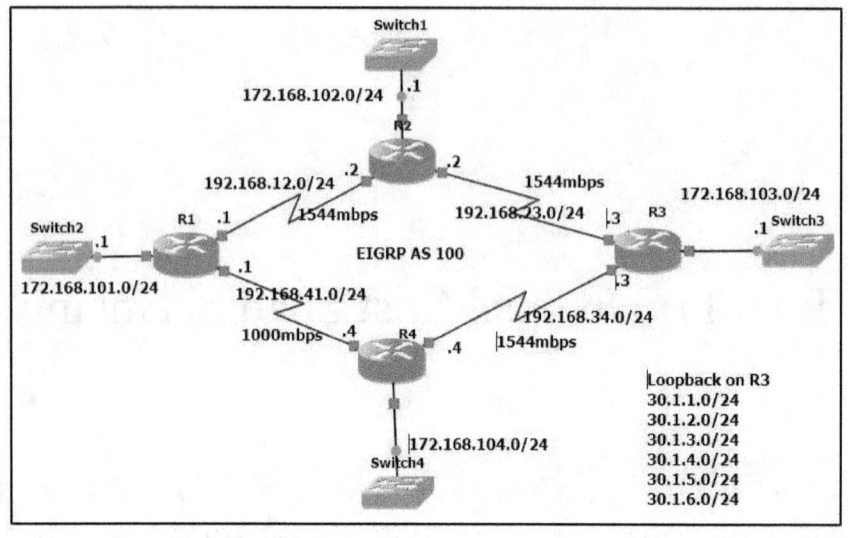

13

LAB 12: OSPF Authentication

Task: To configure type-1 authentication between R1 and R2, which authenticates are OSPF neighbors.

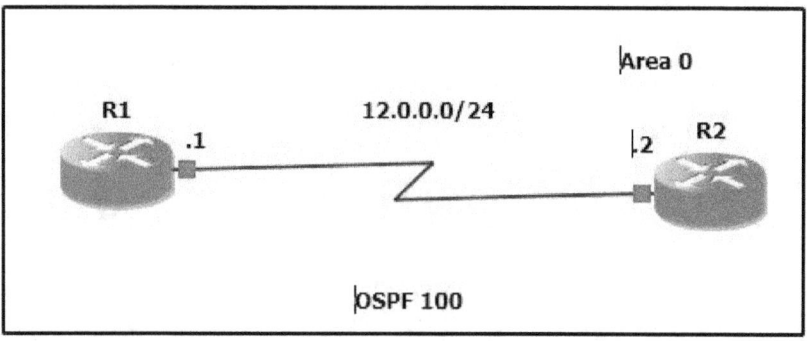

14

LAB 13: MD5 Authentication

Task: To configure type-2 authentications between R1 and R2. Also verify the configuration.

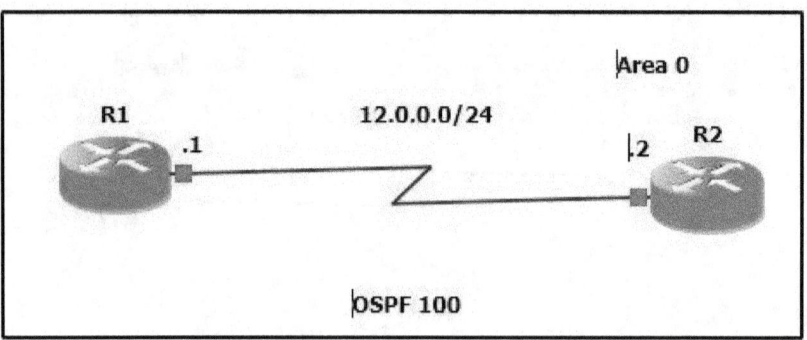

15

LAB 14: OSPF Point-to-Point Network

Task: To configure neighborship over frame-relay point-to-point subinterfaces and verify the configuration.

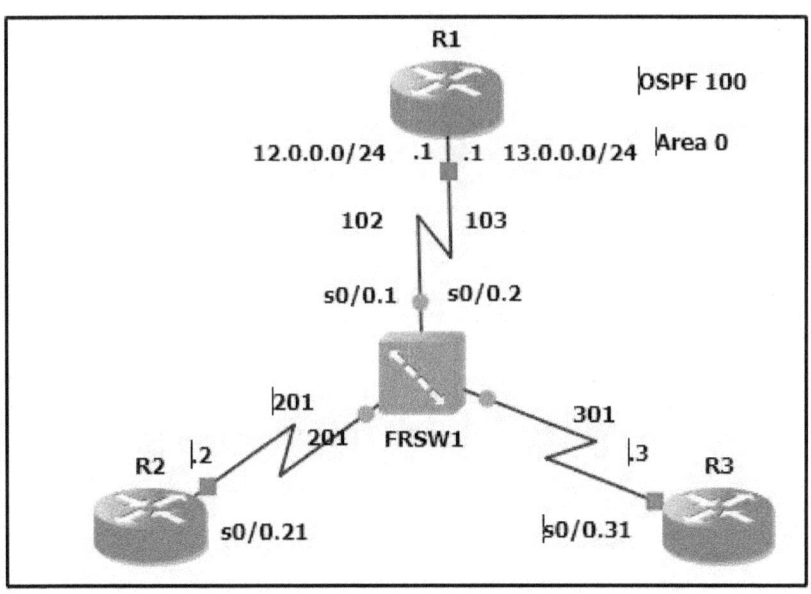

16

LAB 15: OSPF Broadcast Network

Task:

1. To configure OSPF broadcast network type over Frame-Relay hub and spoke network and to verify DR and BDR.
2. To configure spoke routes so that they never participate in DR and BDR elections.

LAB 15: OSPF BROADCAST NETWORK

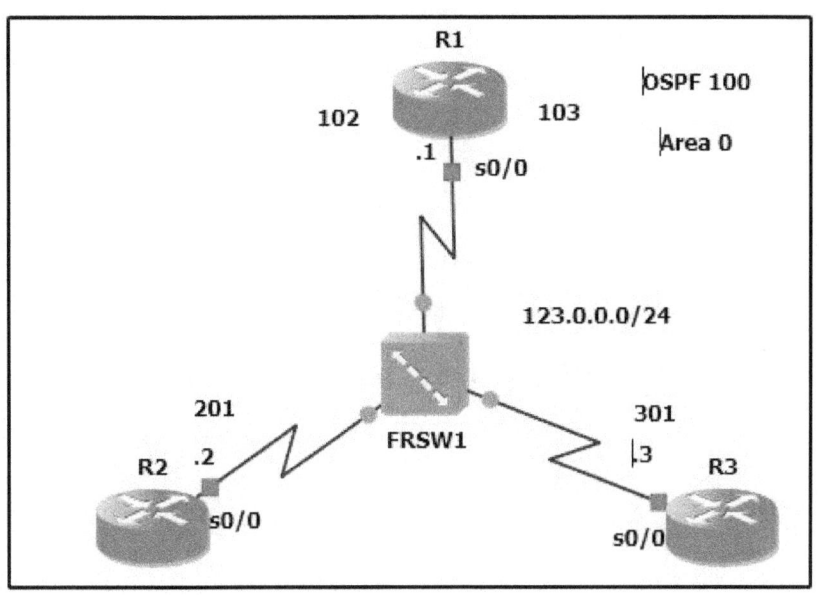

17

LAB 16: OSPF Non-Broadcast Multi Access (NBMA) network

Task: To configure OSPF Non-Broadcast Multi-Access network on Frame Relay and to verify the configuration.

LAB 16: OSPF NON-BROADCAST MULTI ACCESS (NBMA) NETWORK

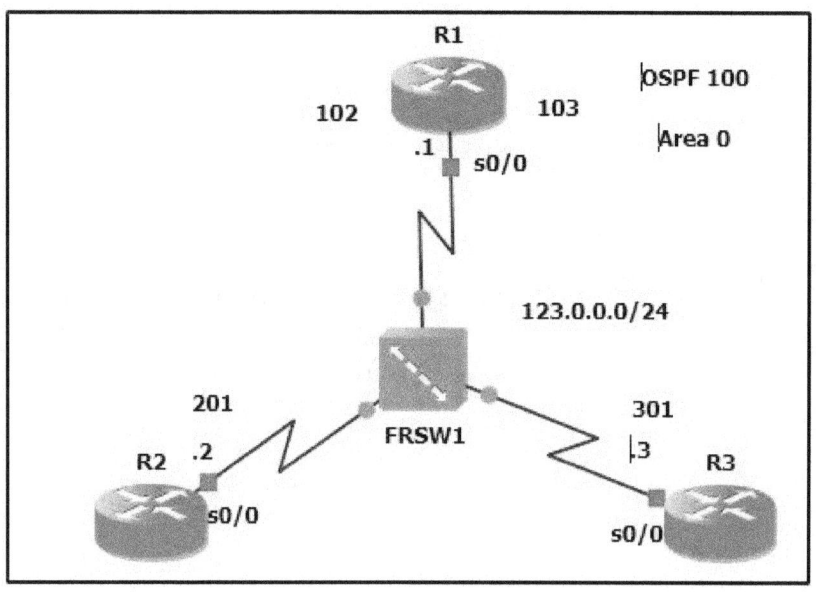

18

LAB 17: OSPF point to Multipoint network

Task: To configure point to multipoint network on Frame Relay and verify the configuration.

LAB 17: OSPF POINT TO MULTIPOINT NETWORK

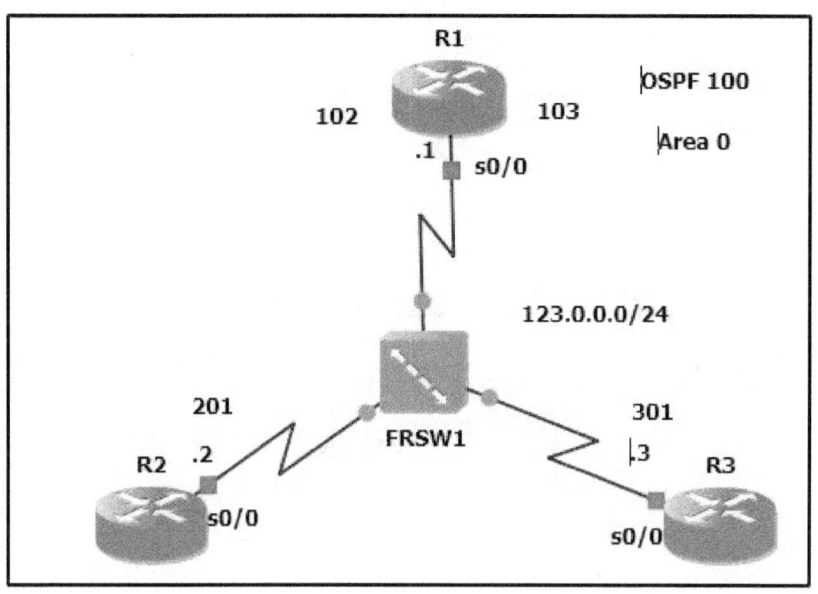

19

LAB 18: Configure OSPF Point-to-Multipoint Non-Broadcast Network

Task: To configure point-to-multipoint network in frame relay and verify the configuration.

LAB 18: CONFIGURE OSPF POINT-TO-MULTIPOINT NON-BROADCAST...

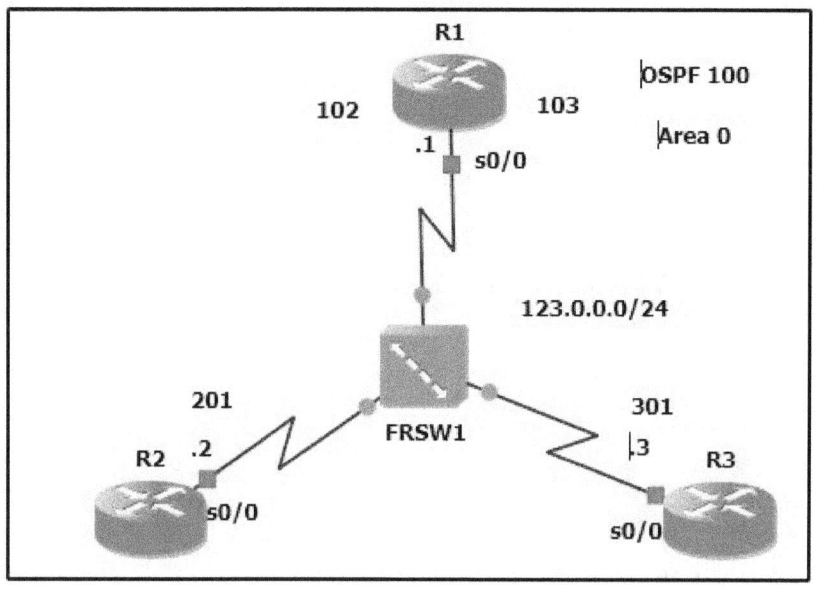

20

LAB 19: OSPF metric tuning

Task:
The best route for the network 172.168.30.0/24 of R3 from R1 is via R2. The task is to make the route via R4 and R5 which is best for the network 172.168.30.0/24 of R3.

Task: To configure the metric values and to make the path via R4 and R5 as the best path for the network of R3 and R1.

1. Change Reference bandwidth
2. Changing cost

LAB 19: OSPF METRIC TUNING

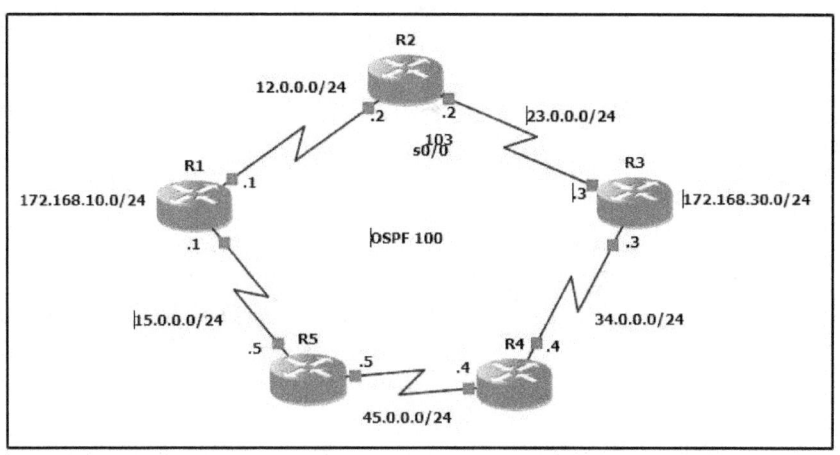

21

LAB 20: OSPF Stub and totally stub area

Task:

1. To configure Area 2 as a stub area and verify its effect on the network.
2. To configure Area 2 as a totally stub area and verify its effect on the network.

LAB 20: OSPF STUB AND TOTALLY STUB AREA

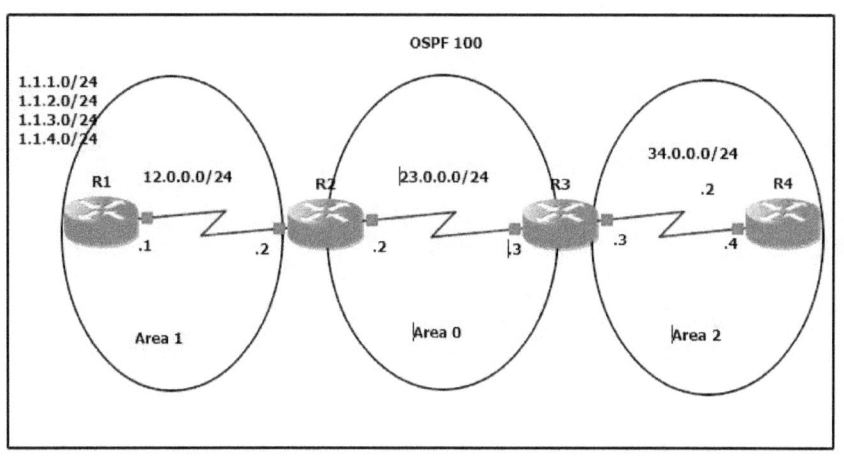

22

LAB 21: NSSA and Total NSSA

Task:

1. To Configure area 1 as a NSSA and to verify its effect on the network.
2. To configure area 1 as a totally NSSA and to verify its effect on the network.

LAB 21: NSSA AND TOTAL NSSA

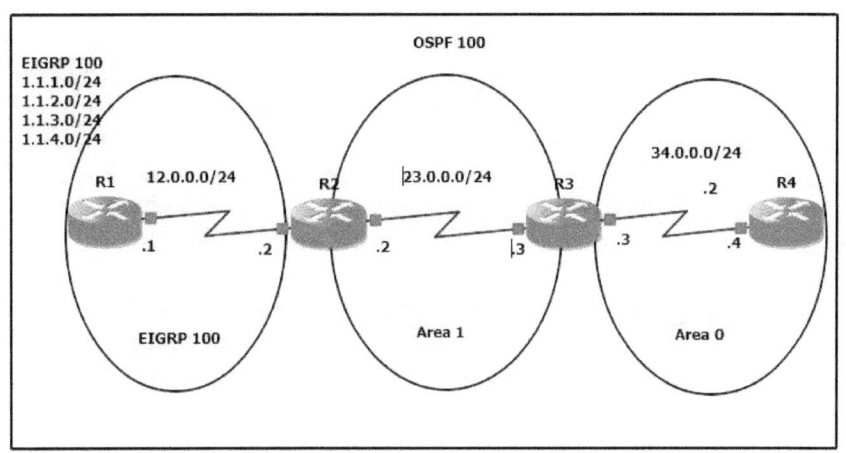

23

LAB 22: Summarization at ABR

To configure summarization at NB (which is ABR). This will make all the branches of NB (NBE,, NSSC AND NBT) receive the routes of the other branches in a summarized manner.

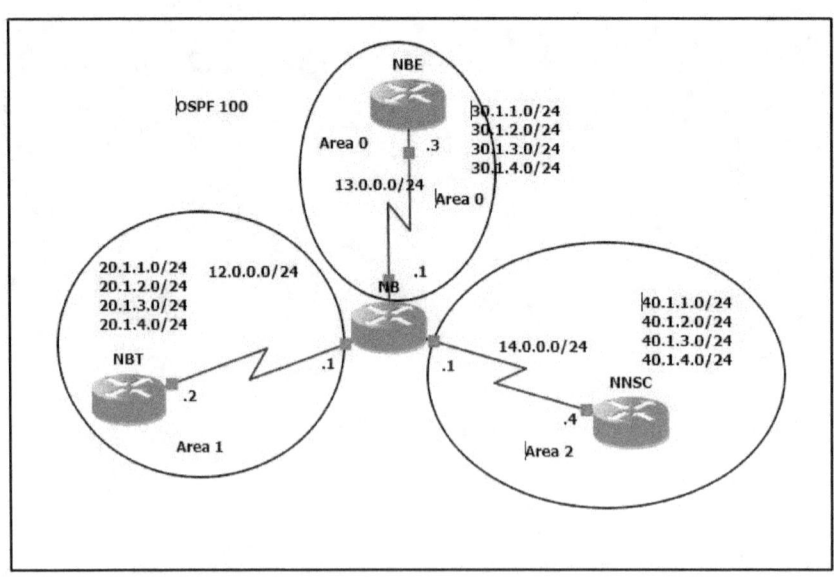

24

LAB 23: Summarization at ASBR

Task: To configure summarization at NBT. Summarization is configured on a ASBR router i.e NBT which will make all the other branches of NB. This will make these branches receive routes of NBTCLIENT in a summarized manner.

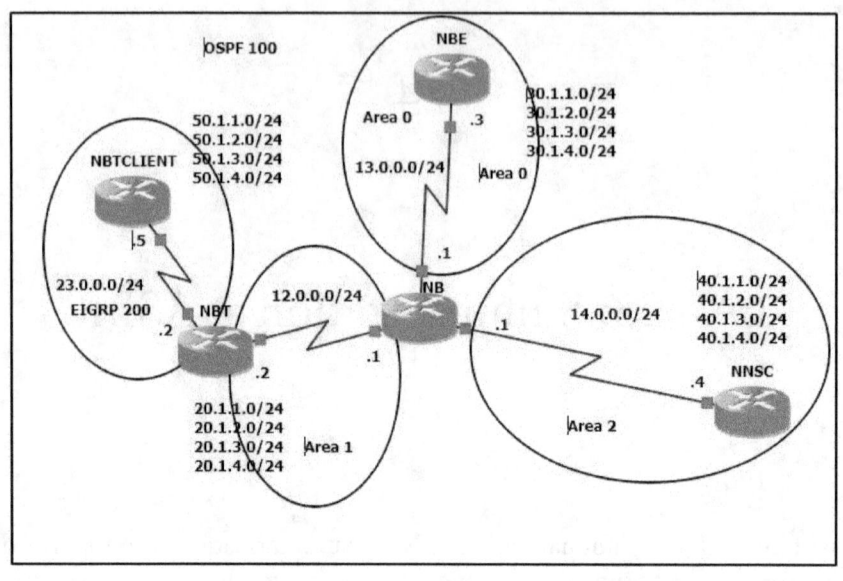

25

LAB 24: Default Routing in OSPF

TASK: To configure default routing at NBT in order to perform routing between OSPF and EIGRP domain. Condition is that OSPF routes must be redistributed under EIGRP domain.

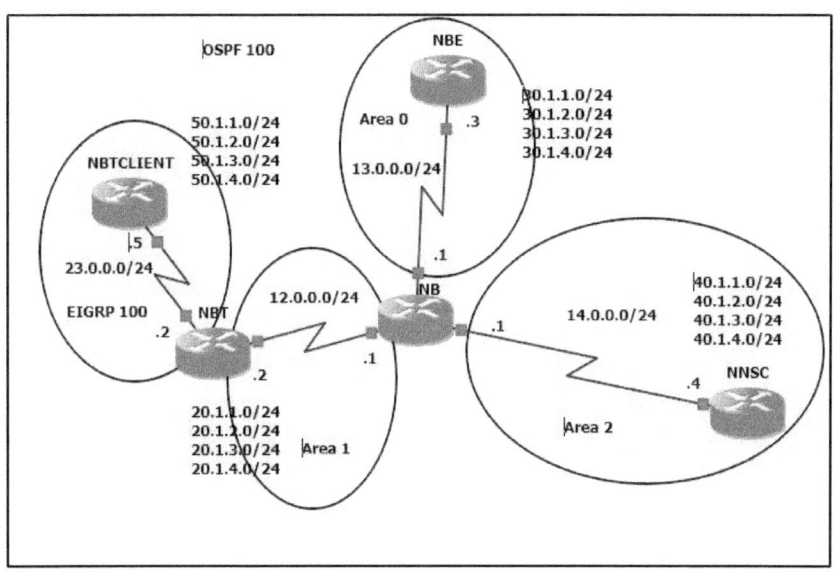

26

LAB 25: OSPF Virtual link with no authentication.

Task: Configure a virtual link between R2 and R3 without using authentication. This virtual link connects Area 2 to Area 0, which is the backbone area.

LAB 25: OSPF VIRTUAL LINK WITH NO AUTHENTICATION.

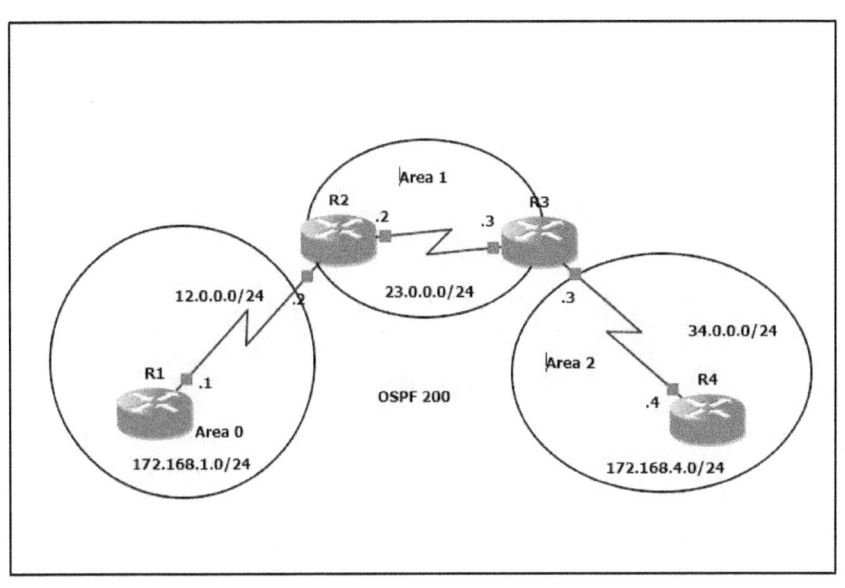

27

LAB 26: OSPF Virtual link with authentication.

Task: Configure a virtual link between R2 and R3 without using authentication. This virtual link connects Area 2 to Area 0, which is the backbone area.

LAB 26: OSPF VIRTUAL LINK WITH AUTHENTICATION.

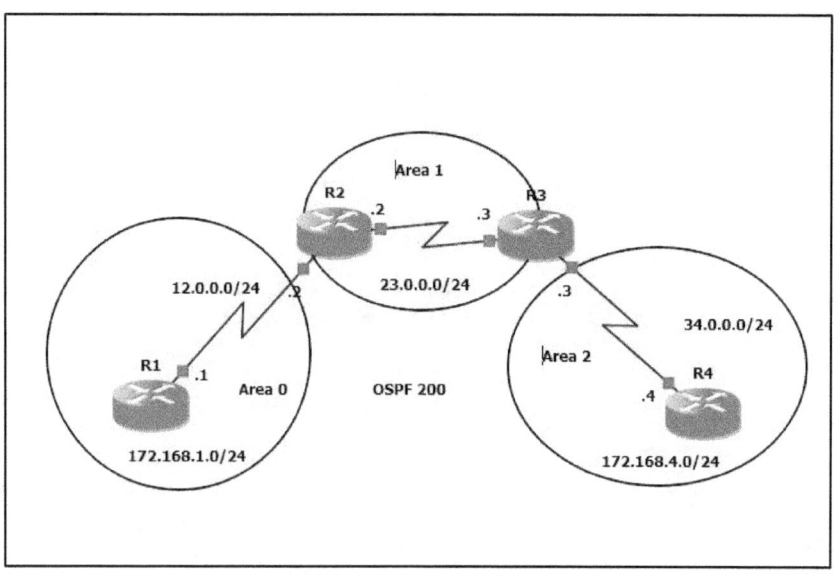

28

LAB 27: OSPF (NNSA)

Task:

1. To configure OSPF area 1 as NSSA.
2. To redistribute loopback 0 interface of R4 into OSPF area 1.
3. To ensure router R3 is the router performing the translation from LSA 7 to type 5 into area 0.

LAB 27: OSPF (NNSA)

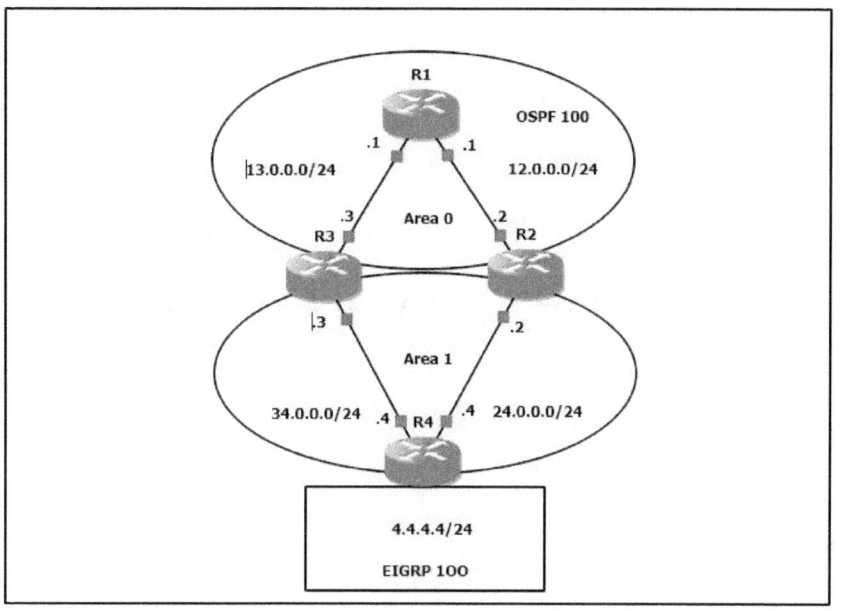

29

LAB 28: OSPF Manual Configuration

Task:

1. To configure OSPF on both the routers, using following policy: On router NB: loopback 0 should be in area 0.
2. On router NB: Create 4 loopbacks:

L1: 10.0.0.1/24
  L2: 10.0.0.2/24
  L3: 10.0.0.3/24
  L4: 10.0.0.4/24

To advertise these networks into OSPF, without using "network" command to achieve this.

1. Take a look at the routing table of router NBT, all the 4 networks should be present in the routing table and must be reachable.
2. To change the area type of area 1 so that these 4 networks are no more present in the routing table of NBT.

LAB 28: OSPF MANUAL CONFIGURATION

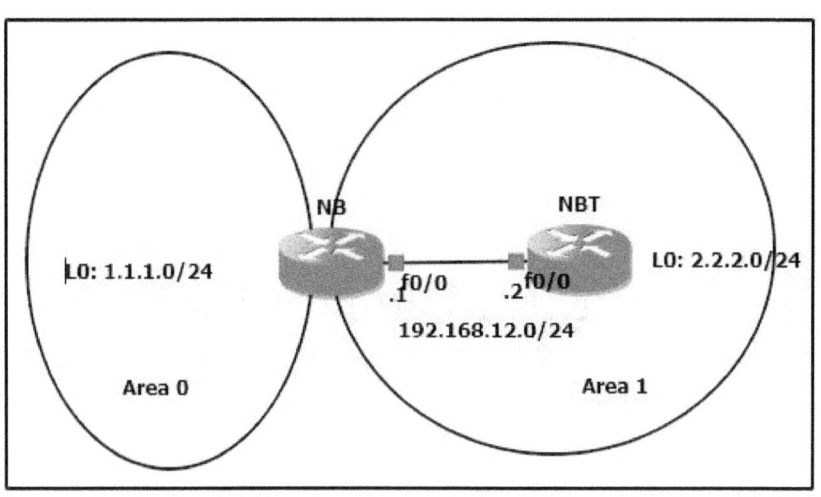

LAB 29: Redistribution of EIGRP into OSPF

Task:

1. To configure OSPF on router NBT and NNSC and only advertise networks 192.168.13.0/24 and 192.168.23.0/24.
2. To redistribute EIGRP information into OSPF on router NBT.
3. Do a traceroute from router NBT or NNSC to network 3.3.3.0/24. In the traceroute output, it can be noticed that it is not using most of the optimal path. Fix the problem so that the router NNSC uses most of the optimal path

LAB 29: REDISTRIBUTION OF EIGRP INTO OSPF

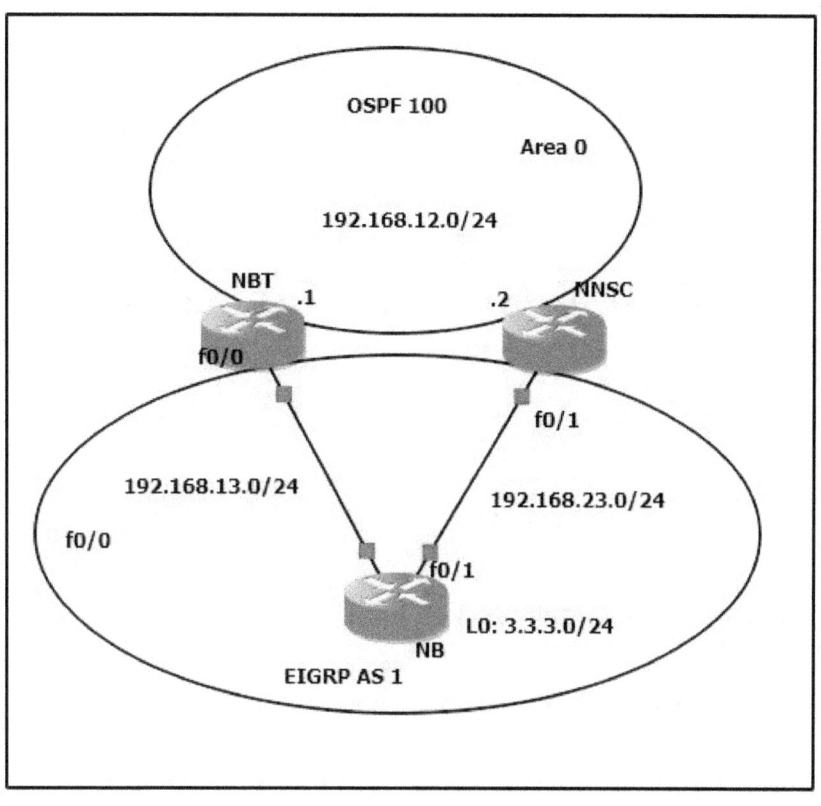

31

LAB 30: EIGRP over Frame-Relay

Task:

1. Configure EIGRP 100 over Frame-Relay
2. Disable FR inverse ARP.
3. Ensure loopback of East and West ping.

LAB 30: EIGRP OVER FRAME-RELAY

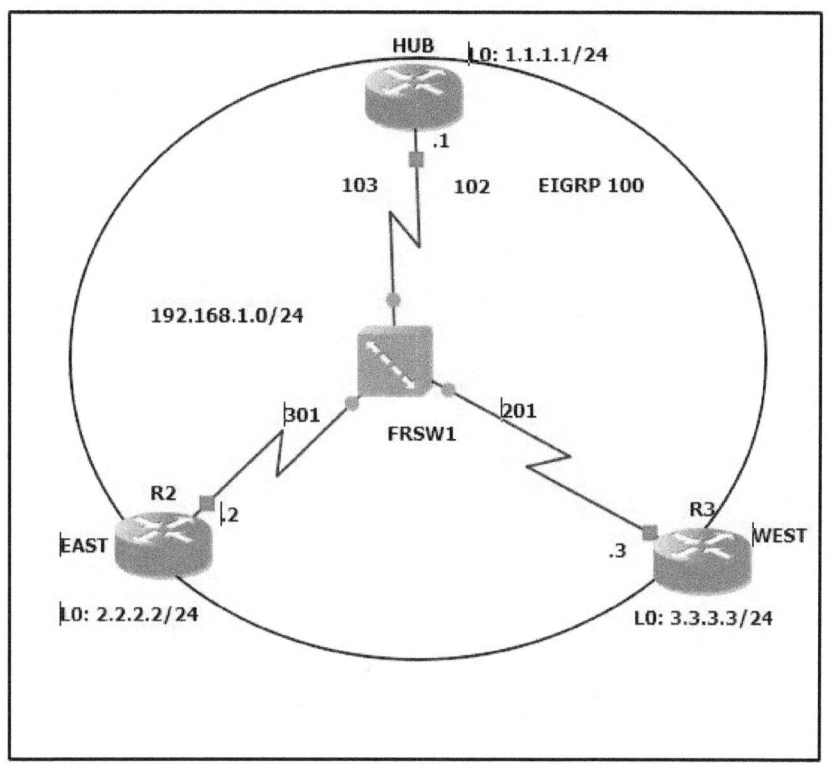

32

LAB 31: EIGRP and OSPF

Task:

1. Configure EIGRP 100 and OSPF as shown in the topology.
2. Ensure that R6 can ping the loopback networks of R4 via OSPF only. In the routing table of R6, the route for network 4.4.4.4/24 should be present.

LAB 31: EIGRP AND OSPF

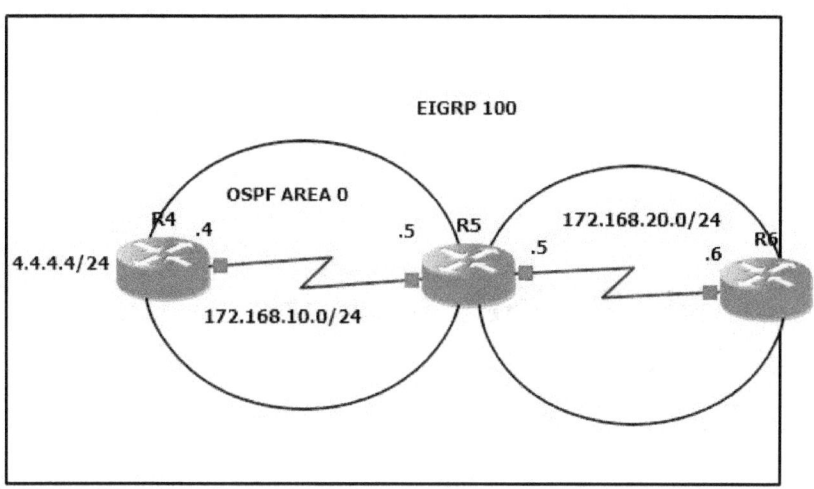

33

LAB 32: OSPF over Frame Relay

Task:

1. Configure OSPF network over frame relay.
2. Create a virtual link between area 34.
3. Advertise loopbacks with their exact masks.
4. Configure neighborship between R2 and R3.
5. Ping from loopback0 OF R4 to 1.1.1.1/24

LAB 32: OSPF OVER FRAME RELAY

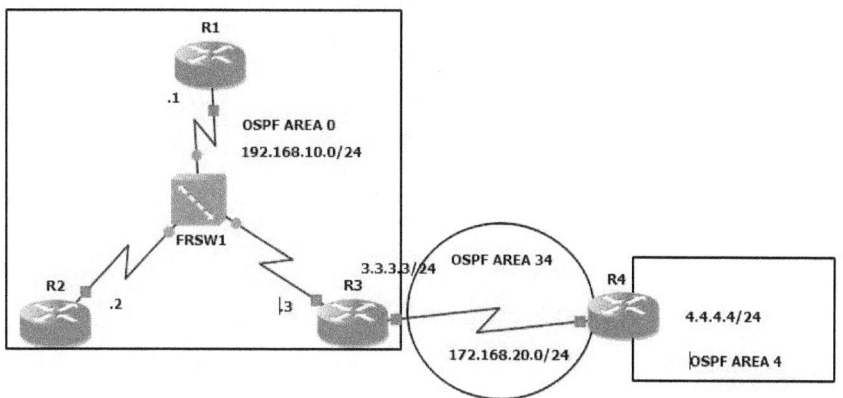

34

LAB 33: OSPF Type

Task:

1. Configure IP addresses and OSPF as shown in the topology.
2. Redistribute networks (loopbacks on R1) into OSPF without using the network command.
3. Change the area type for Area 1 so that you cannot see 4 networks anymore in the routing table, but only the default route.
4. Create a loopback on R3 as shown in the topology. Redistribute this loopback network in OSPF and ensure this loopback.network should ping R1 loopback.

LAB 33: OSPF TYPE

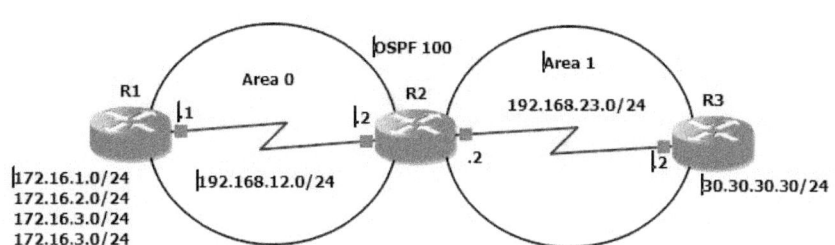

35

LAB 34: Source Based Routing

Task:

1. To configure the topology as shown in the figure.
2. Look up the routing table of R1 and verify the routing table preferred by the network 4.4.4.4/24.
3. Create loopbacks on R1.
4. Configure source-based routing such that if you ping from LB1 to R4's loopback, the RIP path must be preferred over any other.

LAB 34: SOURCE BASED ROUTING

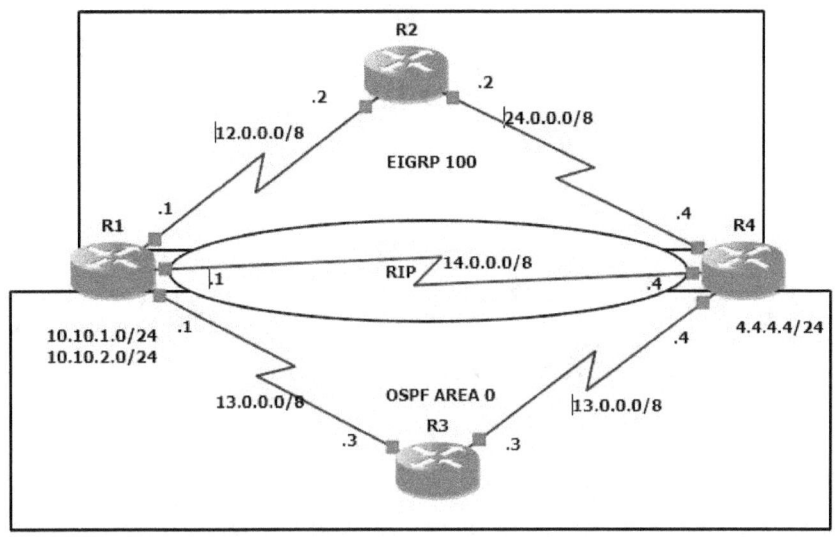

36

LAB 35: EIGRP over Frame-Relay using point-to-multipoint

Task:

1. Configure EIGRP 100 and 300 as shown in the topology.
2. Create loopbacks on R2, R4, and R7
3. Configure a path from R7 to R2 via R3, with RIP as the successor and other paths as feasible successors. Use reliability as a metric.
4. Configure EIGRP 300 over Frame-Relay using point-to-multipoint subinterfaces.

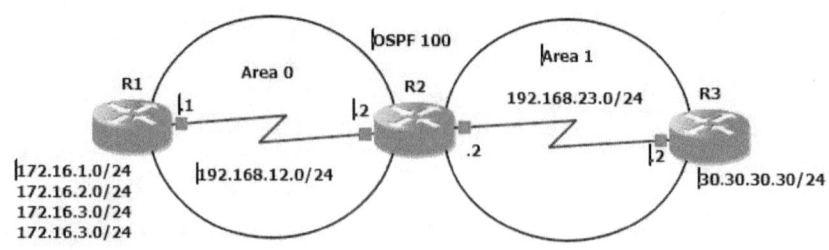

37

LAB 36: BGP

Task:

1. Configure iBGP in AS1 and eBGP between AS1 and AS2.
2. TO ensure AS1 will use the link between R3 and R4 to send the traffic.

Note: Use MED attribute for doing this task. Also, find if there is any other attribute which can be used to accomplish this task or not.

HANDS-ON LAB EXERCISES FOR CISCO NETWORKING BEGINNERS

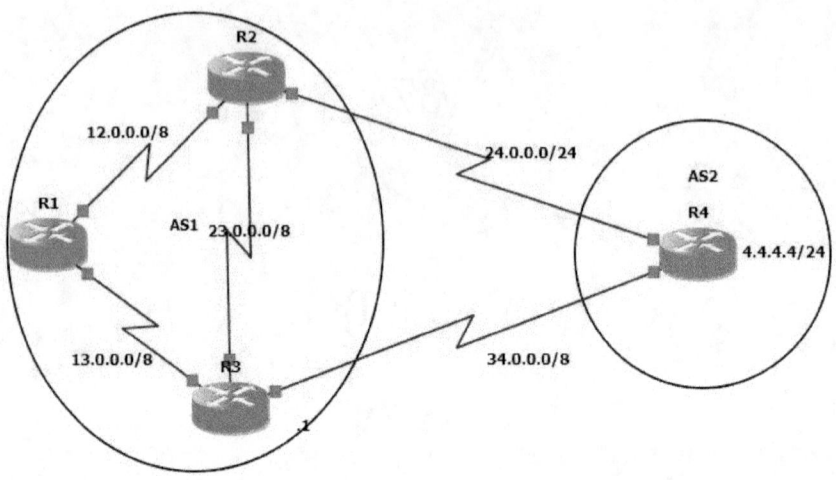

38

LAB 37: Redistribution to OSPF

Task:

1. To configure EIGRP 100 and OSPF as shown in the topology.
2. To create a loopback 7.7.7.7/24 on R7.
3. To redistribute the route received from R7 into the OSPF domain on R5 and R6.
4. To configure redistribute in such a way that R1 will get the routes from both the sides in its routing table.

Note: Use default metric type E2.

HANDS-ON LAB EXERCISES FOR CISCO NETWORKING BEGINNERS

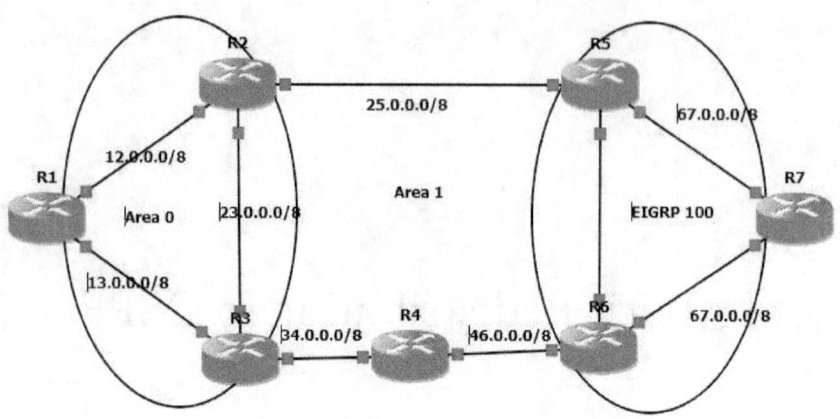

LAB 38: RIP over FRAME RELAY

Task:

1. To configure RIP over Frame Relay
2. To configure PPP and CHAP authentication with password "CISCO" between R9 and R11
3. Ping from R11 loopback to R8 loopback.

HANDS-ON LAB EXERCISES FOR CISCO NETWORKING BEGINNERS

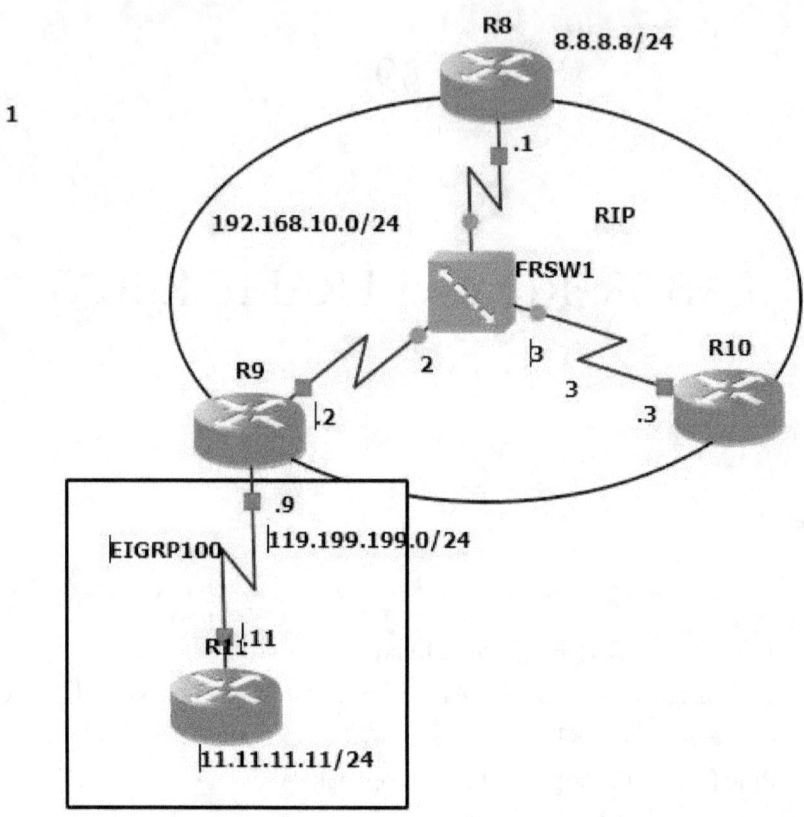

40

LAB 39: EIGRP SUCCESSOR AND FEASIBLE

Task:

1. Configure EIGRP 100.
2. Check for successor and feasible successor for the loopback of R16 in the routing table.
3. Configure path via R15 as a successor using variance

HANDS-ON LAB EXERCISES FOR CISCO NETWORKING BEGINNERS

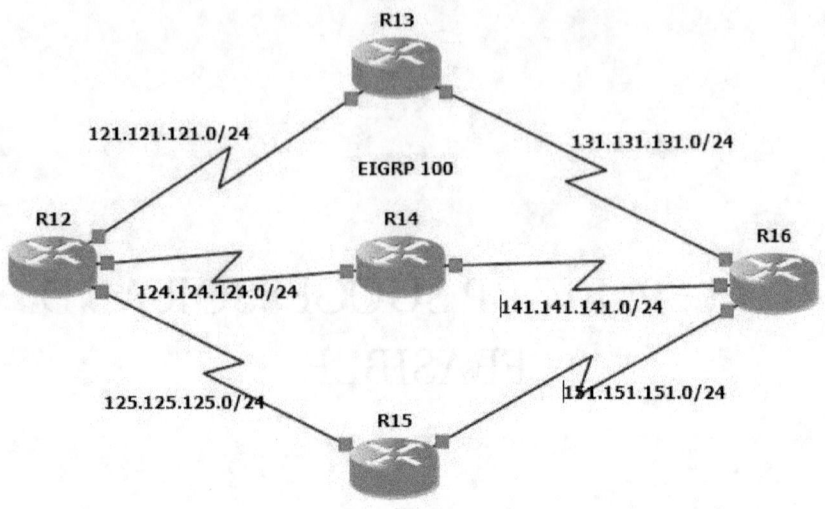

11.11.11.11/24

41

LAB 40: OSPF NSSA And Redistribution

TASK:

1. Configure OSPF as shown in the network.
2. To verify FULL connectivity
3. Configure OSPF area1 as NSSA
4. Redistribute loopback 1.1.1.1/24 on R12 IN OSPF
5. Look up in the routing TABLE of R16

HANDS-ON LAB EXERCISES FOR CISCO NETWORKING BEGINNERS

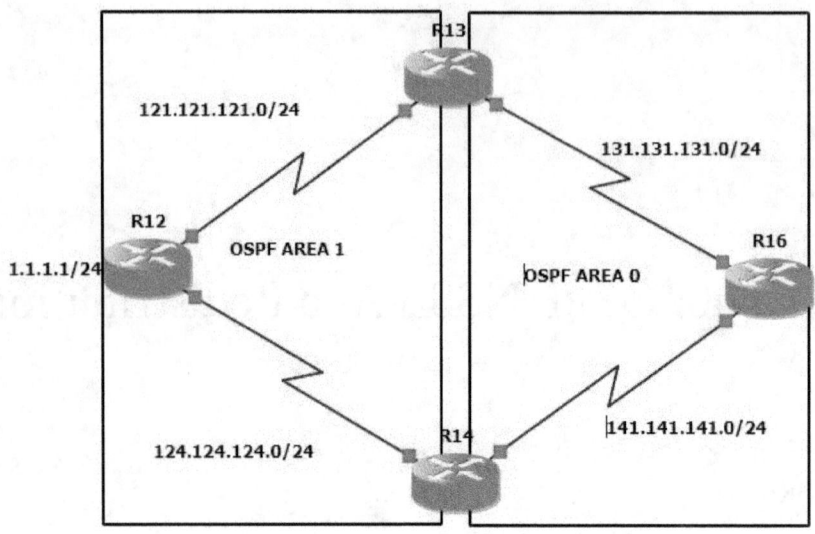

LAB 41: RIPv2

Task:

1. Configure RIP as shown in the figure.
2. Use RIP version 2.
3. Configure authentication between R1 and R2 and between R2 and R3.
4. Configure timers in such a way that convergence becomes 6 times faster.
5. Use the debug command to see the effect.

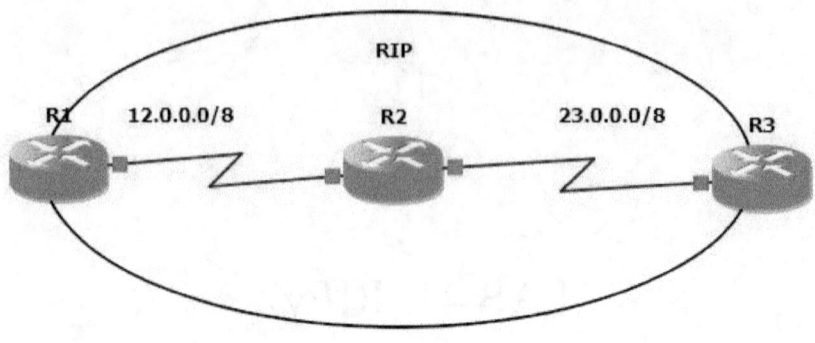

11.11.11.11/24

43

LAB 42: RIP, EIGRP Redistribution

TASK:

1. Configure EIGRP and RIP as shown in the figure
2. Perform redistribution
3. Create summary router on R8 for the loopback and there routes must be reachable to R4 via R6

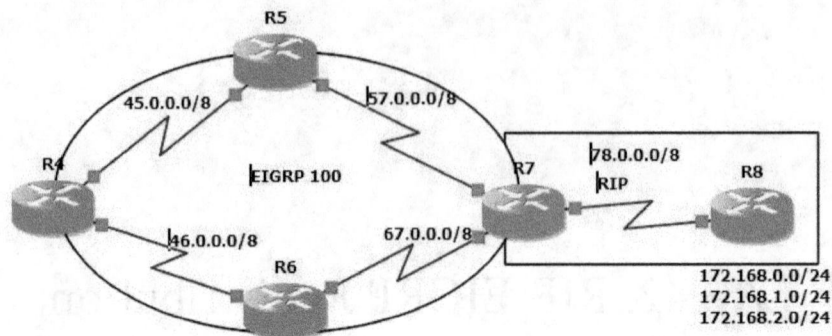

44

LAB 43: OSPF ROUTE

Task:

1. Configure OSPF on all the routers and configure the areas as specified in the topology.
2. Configure R2, so that R4 does not receive the routes of R1 in its routing table.

Note : Route filtering is not allowed

HANDS-ON LAB EXERCISES FOR CISCO NETWORKING BEGINNERS

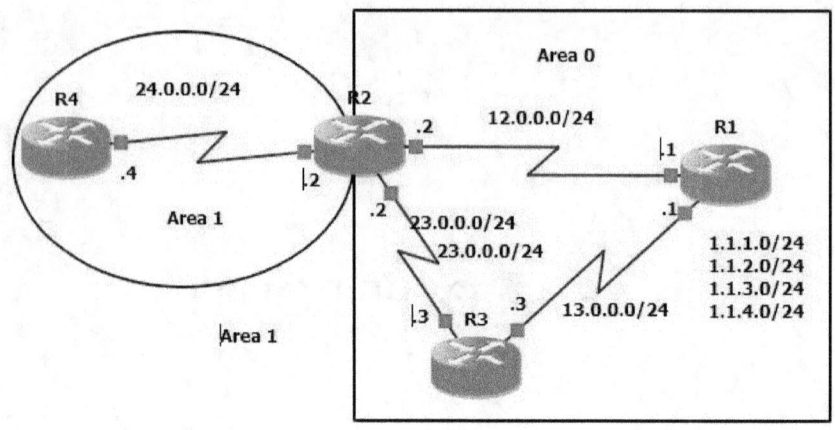

LAB44: VLAN (VIRTUAL LAN)

Task:

Configure two VLANS and name them as NBT AND NNSC on both the switches, Also assign switchportFa1/0/1 and FA1/0/2 to VLAN NBT and switchportFa1/0/3 and Fa1/0/4 to NNSC.

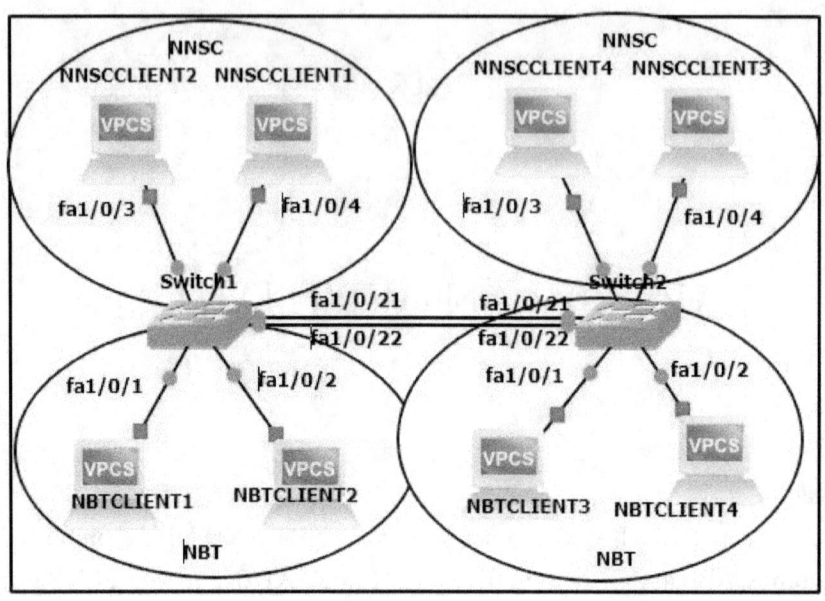

LAB 45: Trunking with ISL encapsulation

Task:

1. configure an ISL trunk between Switch 1 (SW1) and Switch 2 (SW2) using port Fa0/21 and Fa0/22 while following the following policy:
2. On Sw1: the port on switch1 should be configured into permanent trunking mode and they should negotiate to convert the neighboring interface into trunk.
3. On SW2: Ports should actively participate to convert the link into a trunk.

HANDS-ON LAB EXERCISES FOR CISCO NETWORKING BEGINNERS

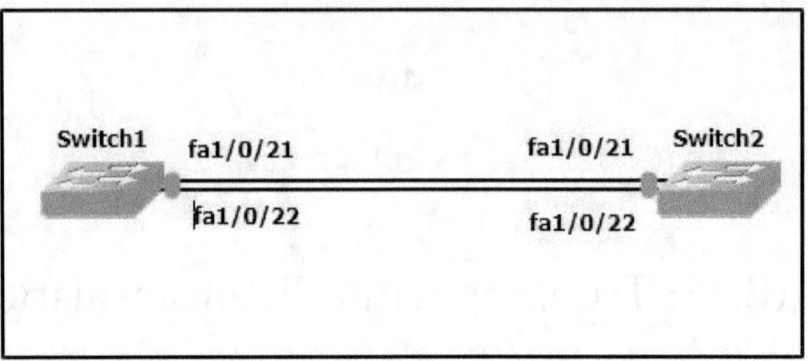

47

LAB46: Trunking with ISL encapsulation using Dynamic desirable modes on both switches

Task: Configure trunk in between both the switches. The port should be configured such that these ports negotiate to convert neighboring interface into ISL trunk.

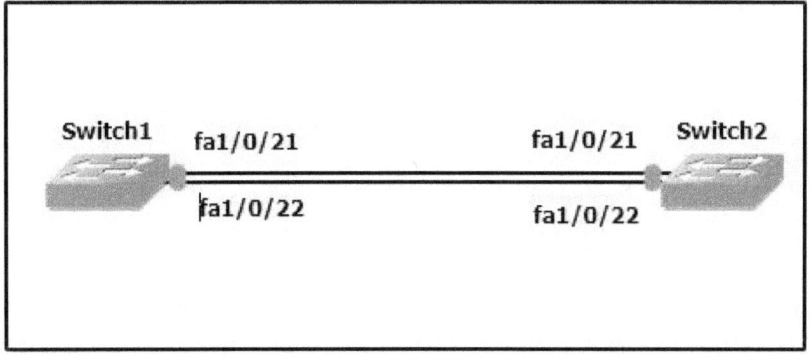

www.ingramcontent.com/pod-product-compliance
Lightning Source LLC
Chambersburg PA
CBHW071949210526
45479CB00003B/872